Esto Perpetua:

THE CLUB OF DR. JOHNSON
AND HIS FRIENDS,
1764-1784

There is no contemporary representation of a meeting of The Club. This 1851 engraving by D. George Thompson after a painting by James E. Doyle, entitled *A Literary Party at Sir Joshua Reynolds'*, presents a scene not unlike one of the meetings. The seated figures are, from left to right, Boswell, Johnson, Reynolds, Garrick, Burke, Paoli, Burney, T. Warton, and Goldsmith.

Esto Perpetua:

THE CLUB OF DR. JOHNSON AND HIS FRIENDS, 1764-1784

by LEWIS P. CURTIS *and* HERMAN W. LIEBERT

ARCHON BOOKS
1963

Library of Congress Card Number: 63-23246

Printed in the United States of America

NOTE

The 250th anniversary of the birth of Samuel Johnson in 1959 occasioned a number of addresses, exhibitions, and publications.

Among these were two talks at the Grolier Club in New York, related to an exhibition of books and manuscripts of members of that circle founded in 1764 which is sometimes called The Literary Club or Johnson's Club, but more accurately The Club.

The members of The Club were intellectually pre-eminent in their own age, and formed an aristocracy of the mind that has perhaps never been equalled in the annals of man binding himself to his peers in a single sodality.

NOTE

In one of these talks about The Club, both here first published, Mr. Curtis, Associate Professor of History at Yale University, incisively examines the nature of the intellectual aristocracy in the age of Johnson. In the other, Mr. Liebert, Librarian of the Beinecke Rare Book and Manuscript Library at Yale, describes the texture of The Club and its members.

The title repeats the motto of The Club: *Esto Perpetua, May it last forever.*

INTELLECTUAL ARISTOCRACY IN EIGHTEENTH-CENTURY ENGLAND

BY L. P. CURTIS

From the whole to the parts — such was the direction which eighteenth-century philosophers took when bent upon analysis. Let us imitate them by breaking down an unknown whole, intellectual aristocracy. What does the term mean? We should not encounter difficulty in reaching the particles that compose the word 'intellect' since both Aristotle and Jacques Barzun are agreed that the word means a capacity for precision of statement. Not, of course, that either thinker made precision absolute or as simple as taking a book off a shelf. For Aristotle there were limits to what a man might know precisely. 'It is the mark of an educated man,' he wrote, 'to look for precision in each class of things just so far as the nature of the subject admits.'[1] For Barzun, who sees phenomena in the historical process as the outcome of human activity, intellect is a tradition consciously maintained by society, a 'tradition of explicitness and energy, of inquiry and debate, of public, secular tests and social accountability', satisfying our need for 'orderly and perspicuous expression, which may lead to common belief and concerted action'.[2] It is a tradition chiefly Western. In England intellect has meant 'brains'. In consequence, the English intellectual could be Sir Robert Walpole no less than his son Horace, or Josiah Wedgwood[3] or his grandson Darwin.

How define 'aristocracy'? We must, I think, be careful to establish a definition of the word that fits English facts. Aristotle's definition is therefore acceptable. He called aristocracy 'government of the best'; its guiding principle was virtue, and by virtue he meant 'a state of character concerned with choice, lying in a mean'.[4] Virtue included courage, honor, temperance, pride, and magnanimity. To be virtuous in this classical sense a man must always walk the 'knife-edge' between extremes – whence the ideal of moderation so attractively exemplified by Lord Falkland and his friends at Great Tew in the days before the Civil Wars, or by Locke or by Chesterfield when he quoted Horace to his bastard son: 'The sure characteristic of a sound and strong mind is, to find in everything those certain bounds, *quo ultra citraque nequit consistere rectum.*'[5] But shall we say that Aristotle's definition of aristocracy as 'government of the best' applied to statesmen like Harley, Bolingbroke, Newcastle, or North? Probably not. In reality, Aristotle's concept of oligarchy described the form of English government in the eighteenth century, but, then, so did his concept of aristocracy. To call the intellectuals an aristocracy is to admit two presuppositions about them: they governed other men's minds by means of persuasion or by Johnsonian blows and knocks; and for the most part they were free of those attributes which Aristotle attached to oligarchy: the aristocracy to which they belonged had no property qualifications and only trifling signs of co-optation. A man entered the English intellectual aristocracy because he had brains, character, and that measure of good manners which made him socially acceptable. Outwardly, at least, he was expected to conform. He happened to be organized into Europe's great intellectual tradition. He was neither a moral nor an intellectual vagabond.

A second question is in order. What was the place of the intellectual aristocracy in England's social structure? The answer is partly evident. The criteria of brains, character, and acceptable manners placed an intellectual aristocrat among the upper and middle classes, that is, among the peers, the country gentlemen, the upper clergy, and leaders in the other professions. The intellectual aristocrat might belong by birth to any of these groups. Or he might be recruited into one or more of them. By whatever route he arrived, he might almost always know that he was 'in' – a member of what we now recognize as England's governing class.

Now in point of merit the class which governed Britain during the eighteenth and nineteenth centuries was almost unique in modern history. The only parallel was the class which produced the American founding fathers. Indeed, the English governing class of those two hundred years was at once the most talented, the most successful, the most high minded, liberal, and intellectually vigorous and creative, and withal the most engaging and respected of any governing class within this era. The class was composed of two wings – the political and the non-political. Often the parts were interchangeable. The whole class governed not only as members of Parliament, ministers of State, lawyers and judges, but as clergymen, officers in Army and Navy, as higher civil servants, local magistrates, as traders, gentlemen farmers, and orators, writers, artists, and scientists.

Together they formed an open aristocracy. That they did so is perhaps the most revolutionary and important factor in English history. The governing class was not a caste at birth; it was not maintained by a closed system. As Tocqueville shrewdly remarked, 'The French wish not to have superiors. The English wish to have inferiors'.[6] Snobbishness, in short, was never more democratic. You could go up the social ladder and you could go down, even as the Catechism advised and by implication warned. That state of life to which God had called Elizabeth's Lord Treasurer Burghley differed significantly from the station of his yeomen ancestors. George II's Lord Chancellor, the Earl of Hardwicke, was the son of a provincial solicitor. Of two Members of Parliament in the reign of George III one had once tended cows and the other had been a waiter at White's; both were knighted. Humphrey Davy, the scientist, was the son of a poor Methodist; yet he rose to fame, fortune, and a baronetcy. The banker Thomas Coutts became the intimate of royal dukes and married his three daughters into the top drawer of English society. That the English open aristocracy has been an abiding and revolutionary tradition is further seen in the elevation to the House of Lords in the twentieth century of Sidney Webb and Herbert Morrison, as well as a miner's son, a former shop assistant, a Union secretary who had once been a newsboy, and even a teacher. In the eighteenth century, no less than today, the criteria of membership in the class were notably casual — birth, of course, and wealth, merit, manners, and seemingly the ability to be amusing. Birth was indeed important, and some people could be vastly exclusive. But it did happen, as Defoe noticed, that there were bred gentlemen as well as born gentlemen.

The structure of the governing class had three primary advantages: in spite of mute inglorious Miltons careers were fairly open to talent, notably in the Church, the Law, and the Navy; the very openness of this aristocracy undid the ardor of violent revolutionaries; and the minds of statesmen could readily be seeded by the thoughts of the intellectual aristocrats. How casual and liberal the aristocratic system was, how given to permit the crossing of social barriers is not far to seek: six peers served as pallbearers at the funeral of Sir Isaac Newton; Chesterfield, even if by accident he overlooked Sam Johnson, confessed to his son that he had approached Addison and Pope with as much awe as if he had been with all the princes of Europe;[7] and, to cite an eyewitness, Wraxall said that he had seen Georgiana, Duchess of Devonshire, 'then in the first bloom of her youth, hanging on the sentences that fell from Johnson's lips'.[8] Many English men and women of good birth respected talent as a matter of course.

A matter of course is always a lively tradition. In eighteenth-century England this particular matter of course had several reasons to explain why intellectuals were respected.

In the first place, English humanists of the sixteenth century had succeeded in fusing the life of action and the life of contemplation. Chaucer's Knight and Clerk of Oxenford betokened a separation between action and contemplation that disappeared in those Renaissance individuals of versatility — Raleigh, courtier, buccaneer, colonizer, and historian; Sidney, poet, diplomat, and soldier; or the essayist, philosopher, and Lord Chancellor, Bacon. A cultural revolution, in fine, had come about, in part prepared by the teachings of the humanists, in part directed by the need of the Tudor government to have its principal servants educated men. The ancient universities of Oxford and Cambridge, hitherto occupied in preparing men for the Church, were invaded by troops of well born youths bent upon secular careers either at Westminster or in their own counties – secular careers for which they required a fairly secular education. Their presence in such great numbers at Oxford and Cambridge heightened the fame of the universities, helped to speed the fusion of clerkly contemplation and utilitarian activity, and gave some measure of a common education, and therefore a common outlook, to sons of patricians as well as of plebeians, who together and in spite of social distinctions formed open aristocracies. The gentleman might study arms, horsemanship, dancing, painting, music, and poetry. At the University he studied logic, Greek and Latin rhetoric and classical philosophy, civil law, history both ancient and modern, and natural philosophy.[9] Upon graduating B.A., gentlemanly intellectuals could readily say that they had exposed themselves to a great deal of the best that had been, and was being, lived and thought. They were, as the French say, *engagés:* if some studied to know God, all studied (or were expected to study) to be of benefit to their country. The whole intent of a university education was summed up in a bidding prayer used at Oxford in the reigns of Charles II and James II: the congregation was enjoined, in order 'that there may never be wanting fit and able men to do God service both in Church and State', to 'beg a blessing upon all schools and nurserys of true religion and sound learning especially the two famous universitys of this land that in them and all other places dedicated to Gods service religion and virtue and whatsoever is praiseworthy may ever flourish and abound'.[10] A code prompted certain undergraduates to assume a pose, a pose of doing something with effortless superiority.[11] There was, for the ambition was an ideal, a universality about their learning. Had not Bacon taken all knowledge for his province? The spacious creed of intellectual versatility swept down from the Renaissance into the later years of the nineteenth century. It then split to pieces on the rocks of specialization – not always excusably.

In the eighteenth century the spaciousness of an educational ideal upheld the fused lives of action and contemplation to make the 'courtier' – or anti-courtier – of that day – the gentleman who was an amateur in learning, no matter what his professional status might be – for example, Thomas Whately, a secretary to the Treasury, principal author of the Stamp Act, an authority on gardening, and a writer on Shakespeare. Lord Bristol told his son that 'the education of youth was the best foundation and support of any state'.[12] 'The education of a man like you,' Lord Bolingbroke wrote to a young earl, 'is of no small importance to the commonwealth.'[13] And Boswell, even if he had no thoughts that his son Sandie should serve the State, counselled him to 'continue to get more and more learning, so that you may be enabled to advance yourself in life, or at any rate do credit to your station; and remember always our ancient family for *that* is the capital object.'[14] Landed families were clannish but they were not often boors.

Nor were those boorish Hanoverians, George I and II, devoid of a desire to be patrons of learning. No matter that Pope exclaimed of George II 'How when you nodded, o'er the land and deep/Peace stole her wing, and wrapt the world in sleep'; or that, later on, one of George III's brothers turned to Gibbon and said, 'So I suppose you are at the old trade again – scribble, scribble, scribble!' George I did buy a bishop's private library of 30,000 books and 1800 manuscripts and presented them to the University of Cambridge; he also established the Regius Professorships of Modern History and Languages in the two universities. George II patronized Handel, and his government founded the British Museum. George III established the Royal Academy and appointed Samuel Johnson the professor of ancient literature. He gave Johnson a pension. He collected a great library that passed after his death to the British Museum. 'Farmer George' set up not only the Board of Agriculture but two agricultural experiment stations at Windsor.[15] The tradition of royal patronage has since flourished and broadened. Both Macaulay and Tennyson were rewarded with baronies. Birthday Honors are now given to historians, actors, scientists, and composers.

In promoting respect for trained intellect John Locke was more influential than English kings. They could set examples. But Locke in the most persuasive way bore down on parents with something truly arresting: he argued from psychology. His essay on human understanding was the proof. 'Of all the men we meet with,' he wrote at the beginning of *Some Thoughts concerning Education* (1693), 'nine parts of ten are what they are, good or evil, useful or not, by their education.' The welfare and prosperity of the nation depended so much upon it.

Most to be taken care of was 'the gentleman's calling', since it was 'every man's indispensable duty, to do all the service he can to his country'.[16] Therefore, study. Experience a range of subjects extending from foreign languages through mathematics, civil law, history, and natural philosophy to dancing, fencing, and an assortment of manual arts. Chesterfield had studied Locke. He told his son Philip that the youth's whole career would depend on the success of his studies between the ages of sixteen and twenty-four. Philip must be many-sided, he must be the *omnis homo, l'homme universel.* Philip did not undertake the Grand Tour in order to enjoy himself or to gaze upon scenery, ruins, and other ancient monuments. He went to acquire character — to acquire polish in Courts and salons and to study Greek, Latin, modern languages, useful literature, Grotius, Justinian, all modern history, rhetoric, geometry, and Bougeant and Adami and the *Corps diplomatique,* forms of government, and the commerce of nations and its cause. Dr. Johnson could not have been more insistent than was Chesterfield about what Johnson called 'the difficulty of excellence, and the force of industry . . . labour vigorously continued'.[17] By 1780 education had become 'the rage of the times'.

In truth, the evidence of intellectual aristocracy in the eighteenth century is so abundant that it stamps itself upon our impression of that age. Consider the book collectors: Anne's Lord Treasurer, Robert Harley, and his son, the second Earl of Oxford, assembled the Harleian Library, a collection of 50,000 books and 8000 manuscripts; other great libraries belonged to the third Earl of Sunderland and to his grandson and Johnson's friend, the second Earl Spencer. Richard Heber, who died in 1833, is said to have filled more than five houses with his two to three hundred thousand volumes. More significant in pointing to the habitual regard for learning were the smaller libraries that could be found in most country houses. Consider the antiquaries who loved old books: such a man was Bishop Percy, editor of the *Reliques* and member of The Club. 'He possessed extraordinary knowledge, a zeal for truth, and a critical conscience.' He teased friends to hunt down rare editions, and the friends, some of them obscure, saved those volumes from oblivion 'because they handled them'.[18] Consider, too, those popular *furores:* the *furor architectonicus* which sent Lords Burlington and Leicester to Italy to study the works of the incomparable Palladio and helped drive Lord Verney into bankruptcy; the *furor hortensis* which attracted that brilliant orator and strategist, William Pitt the Elder; or the *furor agrestis* which in the last half of the eighteenth century changed the very landscape and brought the tools of Enlightenment, observation and experiment, to the estates of countless country gentlemen and their tenants.

Government almost sparkled with intellectuals. In Commons sat many eminent jurists, including Blackstone, as well as patrons of learning, literary scholars and scientists; there among the men of letters one might have seen Horace Walpole, 'Ossian' Macpherson, 'Monk' Lewis, and 'Vathek' Beckford. That great architect of equity, Lord Hardwicke, served his king as Lord Chancellor for nineteen years; his most distinguished disciple, Lord Chief Justice Mansfield, raised commercial law almost to an exact science. Perhaps no episode in English history of the eighteenth century reveals more effectively the fusion of action and contemplation than a moment at Lord Granville's in 1763. The most knowing English diplomat of his day, a student of the classics, and patron of men of letters, Granville signed the Treaty of Paris and quoted lines from the *Iliad* in the presence of Robert Wood, M.P. and Under-Secretary of State, who was himself an accomplished Homeric scholar and the explorer of Palmyra and Baalbek.[19]

Clearly the two men were humanists.

Finally, educated families, and more influential than families, the societies and clubs produced intellectual aristocracy. Let us examine the educated families first.

Unfortunately no study of intellectual families in the eighteenth century has, in so far as I know, been made – certainly no study comparable to Noel Annan's essay on 'the' intellectual aristocracy in the nineteenth and twentieth centuries;[20] and for good reason: virtually all of England's most celebrated philosophers and men of letters in the eighteenth century were childless, and Burke's two children died young and unmarried. Moreover, the variety of professions had not yet advanced to the point where they could nourish and support linked generations of Stephens (so far, the Stephens can show five generations of achievement), Macaulays, Arnolds, Trevelyans, Butlers, Potters, Darwins and their cousins Wedgwood.

Yet of highly talented families there were a good many and they may be selected almost at random. From Ireland in the last half of the eighteenth century came the Wellesley brothers. In England flourished their cousins the Wesleys (three generations of them), the Walpoles, Cartwrights, Foxes, Wartons, Burneys, and Gurneys. Hereditary ability, skipping a generation, linked Locke's pupil, eventually the celebrated philosopher and third Earl of Shaftesbury, to his grandfather, Dryden's 'Achitophel', the acute, notorious first Earl. Heredity, skipping two generations, linked the philosopher-statesman, the first Marquess of Lansdowne, to the talents of his great grandfather, the economist Sir William Petty; and the great grandfather of the chemist and physicist, Henry Cavendish, after whom the Cavendish Laboratory at Cambridge was named, was the Revolution Whig, William Cavendish, created for his support of William III first Duke of Devonshire. The second Duke, Henry

Cavendish's grandfather, was chiefly responsible for the Chatsworth Collection of drawings. The descendants of England's most potent 'sire', Sir George Villiers, ran true to type: given to genius and charm, they were either 'mad, bad, and dangerous to know', as Caroline Lamb said of Byron, or they were well balanced and conspicuous or just odd. Villiers blood ran in the veins of the first Duke of Marlborough, the memoirist Lord Hervey, Henry Fielding and his half-brother John (the blind Bow-street magistrate), Elizabeth Chudleigh (tried in the House of Lords for bigamy), the two Pitts and Grafton and Portland (all four of them 'prime ministers'), and in the gorgeous Georgiana, Lady Bessborough, Byron's Caroline, Sarah Lennox and her brood of distinguished Napiers, 'Citizen' Stanhope, Castlereagh, and so on to Grey of Falloden, Bertrand Russell, and Winston Churchill.[21] Villiers blood, as Keynes observed, is the true blood royal of England.[22]

Blood of itself did not make an intellectual aristocrat as readily as did a parent's guidance. The very mood of eighteenth-century upperclass England still lingers in the portrait sketched by his son of Robert Hay Drummond, George III's first Archbishop of York. The Archbishop talked history to his children as a result of his labor to know and his leisure to impart. He was wont to give 'in a perspicuous and engaging manner' 'the great lines of general history, deducing from thence the most useful remarks on government, manners, morals, and religion'; he traced 'particular events and actions to their genuine sources and motives', and he developed with discrimination, while avoiding political prejudice, 'the characters of individuals who had rendered themselves conspicuous on the great stage of life'.[23] Except that he emphasized the truths of divine revelation, the Archbishop in talking history talked pure Gibbon.

As for societies and clubs, they were

part of the national character. 'We are, of all nations,' David Fordyce wrote, 'the most forward to run into clubs, parties and societies, which, by the by, is no ill proof of the sociable turn of our temper . . . We have clubs for trade, musical clubs, clubs for mathematical and philosophical researches, clubs for improvement in the fine arts, clubs for pure diversion and merriment.'[24] Clubs and associations of a much less formal nature had proved irresistible among English intellectuals since the days of Ben Jonson and his circle at the Mermaid and the Lord Falkland's friends at Great Tew. There followed the Royal Society of 1662, the Scriblerus Club, and Bolingbroke's circle at Dawley. At Bowood Shelburne gathered together Richard Price, Joseph Priestly, and the titan of Utilitarian philosophy, Jeremy Bentham. In time Bentham had his own disciples at 'QSP' in Westminster, whence British legislators learned. What does English civilization perhaps owe to dinner tables, especially to the dinner tables of Sir Joshua Reynolds, Lady Holland, and Beatrice Webb? Easily our imaginations can run away with us as we recall the Saints at Clapham, the Lunar Society, the Cambridge Apostles, the Oxford and Cambridge Unions, the Souls, or the Bloomsbury Group distinguished by Virginia Woolf, Clive Bell, Keynes, Lytton Strachey, and E. M. Forster. It is time that our attention return to the most famous of English Clubs – The Club.

There is no need here to recall that The Club was founded by Sir Joshua in 1764, presumably to hear Johnson talk, that the original members numbered eight, that by 1776 it met for dinner every two weeks, or that on one occasion, in 1825, the prime minister himself, Lord Liverpool, attended a meeting and dined alone. Nor is there need to remark upon The Club's assembled talent, even genius, in the early years. Yet how illustrious they were and how on the whole they enjoyed each others' company! Who more eminent in lexicography, literary criticism, and good talk than Johnson, or in historical writing than Gibbon, in painting than Reynolds, in poetry than Goldsmith, in the writing of comedies than Sheridan, in political economy than Adam Smith, in acting than Garrick, in parliamentary debate than that dismaying, lovable man Charles Fox, in political philosophy than Burke, and, in biography than Boswell? In those years members of The Club wrote three of the world's greatest books — the *Decline and Fall of the Roman Empire, Reflections on the Revolution in France,* and the *Life of Samuel Johnson.* Johnson did not exaggerate when he suggested that members of The Club could make up the faculty of a college.[25]

Less familiar is appreciation of how representative of the English intellectual aristocracy in the eighteenth century The Club actually was. Let us, for purposes of analysis, confine our attention to the forty-nine men who belonged to The Club between 1764 and 1792, the year of Reynolds's death. Their diverse backgrounds go far to establish the openness of England's aristocracy or governing class. Johnson was the son of a bookseller. Among other members were a duke, the heir to a famous earldom, the great great grandson of Charles II and grandson of a duke, and sons of a livery-stable keeper, a clergyman, a merchant, a coal broker, and a country gentleman. Of the forty-nine members at least thirty-three had attended a university. Some thirty had administrative experience in either Church or State. Four members sat as temporal peers in the English House of Lords, eighteen sat at one time or another in the Commons, six were bishops, seven were lawyers, and one presided over the Royal Society.[26] Such men of practical experience stood in no danger of being mere theorists. They knew the art of the possible.

The diversity of their backgrounds and

experience was enhanced by the diversity of their ages upon first election into The Club. In 1764 Johnson was fifty-five and Beauclerk was twenty-five. Fox became a member at the age of twenty-four, the age at which the younger Pitt was appointed First Lord of the Treasury. Boswell was elected when he was thirty-two and Johnson touching sixty-four. Diversity sprang also from sharp differences of opinion among certain members – for example, Johnson the Utopian Tory could, for all his affection and regard, oppose those two vile Whigs, Burke and Fox; or again, Johnson the Anglican chose not to discuss religion with Gibbon, who at the close of his *Decline and Fall* wrote that 'in the preceding volumes of this history I have described the triumph of barbarism and religion'. Trying, indeed, must have been the meetings of The Club during the American revolution, although less trying than the meeting eight days after the execution of Louis XVI, when Burke's son and Fox did not speak to each other and 'not a word of the martyred king or politics of any kind were mentioned'.[27] But tolerance had its limits: The Club blackballed the pro-Wilkes judge, Lord Camden, and the Evangelical Bishop Porteus. In the nineteeth century The Club passed over those outsiders, Bentham, Byron, Carlyle, John Mill, Disraeli, and Swinburne. The Club was to be composed of clubable men, 'an assembly', as Johnson said, 'of good fellows meeting under certain conditions'.[28]

Out of such diversity, strengthened as it was by the ideal of precise, informed statement, came the 'manly conversation' that Gibbon admired in members of The Club. They agreed, of course, to disagree, and thus they hoped to find truth. Conversation for Johnson meant discussion, not gossip, and sometimes it meant tossing and goring. Close conversation pointed up a man's real abilities; in the best talk a man, as Johnson said, 'put fairly his mind to yours'.[29] There were members who could talk from the many-sidedness which the giants of Tudor days and also Chesterfield admired and which John Mill would hold as an ideal of responsible men. 'Take up whatever topick you please,' Johnson said of Burke, 'he is ready to meet you.'[30] To Johnson's conversation Burke confessed that he owed the best part of his education, even as Fox confessed his similar debt to Burke's. Much to be regretted is loss of what they talked about. Boswell excelled, of course, in reporting dialogue but he made only one principal effort to suggest the talk of members as a group, to wit, the famous entry for April 3, 1778. On that evening the conversation ranged from emigration and oratory in Parliament to the Irish language, books of travel, the nature of man (of course), and outrageous puns.[31]

On that evening, in fine, Club members talked like most other philosophic conversationists throughout the eighteenth century. They talked about this world. But they were far from being worldlings. It is the glory of the scientific revolution of the seventeenth century and its offspring, the eighteenth-century Enlightenment, that intellectual men and women turned once again to the problems of man, his world, and universe. Out of Enlightenment – how casually it was cherished in England where as yet neither Church nor State were targets for more than a handful of Radicals to shoot at – came a common mind, common because of common aims and common presuppositions about the autonomy of nature, progress, and the usefulness of reason and analysis. The eighteenth-century intellectual could display the many-sidedness of Raleigh, Sidney, and Bacon. The elder Pitt delighted in oratory, gardening, and strategy. Johnson was a poet, lexicographer, literary critic, parliamentary reporter, and pamphleteer. No one in the reign of George III surpassed Sir Joseph Banks (elected into The Club in 1778) in the range of his achievements and philosophical interests. He corresponded with the international company of the learned. He had gone round the world with Captain Cook and he had visited Iceland. He promoted expeditions to the Niger and to Australia and was concerned in establishing Chinese tea-plants in India, South American cochineal insects in Asia, South Sea bread-fruit in the West Indies, and Spanish Merinos in England. On his estate in Lincolnshire he was a generous and enlightened agriculturist in a heyday of English farming. His zest for knowledge and the welfare of his country caused him to serve faithfully on government committees, to help in establishing the Royal Horticultural Society and Kew Gardens, and as President of the Royal Society for forty-two years he chose to be a citizen of the learned world rather than the mere subject of a king at war with a host of enemies.[32] If English many-sidedness never reached climax until the advent of Winston Churchill, one point is clear: the intellectuals mostly taught themselves.

They were self-taught amateurs; and they could still communicate together. Learning in the eighteenth century had not yet advanced to the point where men familiar with the humanities cannot understand the scientists and where the scientists do not even pretend to understand each other. 'Perhaps,' Trevelyan has written wistfully, 'no set of men and women since the world began enjoyed so many different sides of life, with so much zest, as the English upper classes' in the later eighteenth century. 'The literary, the sporting, the fashionable and the political "sets" were one and the same'[33] — a fusion of action and contemplation.

None of these intellectuals, moreover, was a system-builder. They were far removed from Descartes and his comprehensive egotism. They did not, on the whole, develop their thought by means of *a priori* reasoning. They learned about truth from experience in Parliament or in the law or in administration and they had learned, too, from their estates, if

Fortune had given them estates, from their laboratories, and from books and talk. They took their cue from the great English empiricists, from Bacon, Newton, and from Locke, who had said that philosophy was 'nothing but the true knowledge of things'.[34] 'Whence,' he asked in a resounding question, 'has it [the mind] all the *materials* of reason and knowledge? To this I answer, in one word, from EXPERIENCE. In that all our knowledge is founded; and from that it ultimately derives itself.'[35] Away, then, with innate ideas and other vain hypotheses. 'Hypotheses', Newton had declared, 'have no place in experimental philosophy.'[36] To reason rightly in philosophy, he continued, a man must infer propositions from the phenomena and, afterwards, render the propositions general by induction. Without observation of phenomena, without experience, and reflection upon experience, a man must be blind and as lost among uncharted seas as a mariner without a compass or sounding-line. 'It is of great use to the sailor,' Locke advised, 'to know the length of his line, though he cannot with it fathom all the depths of the ocean.'[37] Years later, Burke picked up Locke's image to describe his own method of thought: 'I heaved the lead,' he wrote, 'every inch of way I made.'[38] And he confessed that his school had been and was 'the usage of Parliament.' Thus wisdom or principles derived from the observations of phenomena constituted a humanist's science in this age of reason. Small wonder, then, that Bishop Warburton could refer to the study of human nature, Blackstone to the study of law, both Hume and Gibbon to history, and Reynolds to the rules of taste, as 'science'. To be an enlightened philosopher was to be as precise and as scientific as the subject permitted. Few English intellectuals, when contemplating man and society, carried scientism to the extremes that Bentham did.

As Kant said, an enlightened philosopher must dare to know. English intellectuals of the eighteenth century were free men. They used freedom either to preserve or to discover truth by means of enquiry based on observation and experience. Holding such aims, The Club in either Jacobin Paris or Nazi Berlin would probably have been suppressed. The English virtuoso believed in intellectual adventure round and about a conservative moral base. To this goal he held and holds, although for a time in the nineteen thirties the moral base disintegrated, leaving him open to vicious attractions, the Communist or the merely profligate.

Thus from a myriad of particulars the English intellectuals reasoned in order to reach what Johnson called 'the grandeur of generality'. To generalize in the eighteenth century was to yield to an irresistible passion. Had not Newton himself dared to generalize – with momentous results? Generalization, Bertrand Bronson has written, was 'of the utmost importance . . . it was one of the chief ways in which a man transcended his private experience and became adult . . . To generalize was, in fact, to be civilized'.[39] For example, Lord Chesterfield in his letters to his son Philip removed almost all traces of his encounter with the eighteenth century except the philosophical, based as it was on observation of men and manners. Foremost was a man's character, actual or presumptive. Philip Stanhope must have character. The younger Pitt preferred character to office. Lord North confessed that he himself wanted character or 'weight'. Generalization enhanced a man's character in the world by showing that he had made up, if not closed, his mind about the meaning of things and values in human life; in sum, that he was, in Locke's sense of the word, a philosopher. What though the pious Johnson and the sceptic Hume used the same method of reasoning? Johnson could without perplexity lock up his faith in the chapel of his soul and practice induction with the best of them. Like Aristotle himself, such men found 'grandeur' in developing the knowledge of nature.

They studied nature and they studied man in nature. Therefore they appealed to his experience in time. To be sure, as men of the Enlightenment they rarely – except for the great Gibbon – sought man in the mire of historical detail. It was easier and more polite to generalize. For this reason and owing to Enlightenment's scepticism and preoccupation with the recent past, above all with the present, as Professor Douglas has argued, the mightiest age of English antiquities, which had opened with the Restoration, came virtually to an end about the year 1730.[40] Henceforth for another two generations it was fashionable to dismiss the Middle Ages as monkish or barbaric. Yet the despised English antiquarians, no less than historically minded philosophers, had built upon experience. If the antiquarians did not bequeath readable folios to their immediate posterity, they

fostered qualities in the English character

> which have in no small measure been responsible for the greatness of this land. They reflected in the nation a reverence for the past, and during an age of change they taught her to rely upon traditional wisdom rather than novel doctrine . . . they were all concerned to insist, throughout an era of critical transformation, that political structure and public policy must be based upon the essential character of the nation as discovered in its past history.[41]

In this spirit Members of Parliament debated. Johnson, who seems not to have cared much for history other than literary history, also conformed. 'Human experience, which is constantly contradicting theory,' he said, 'is the great test of truth. A system built upon the discoveries of a great many minds, is always of more strength, than what is produced by the mere workings of any one mind, which, of itself, can do little.'[42] Likewise Burke, whose intelligence was so wonderfully sensitive to the import of history: political arrangement, he wrote, 'requires the aid of more minds than one age can furnish . . . There mind must conspire with mind. Time is required to produce that union of minds which can alone produce all the good we aim at. Our patience will achieve more than our force.'[43] Here indeed, given the historical awareness of the nineteenth century, is the mental world in which Newman and, later still, the Webbs moved and had their being. One cannot help surmising that Burke's awareness of history, notably English history as a developing process and matrix of society, ran truer to English assumptions than the contempt for the past that in part prompted those egotists, Bentham, Paine, and Godwin, to be philosophers.

For Burke, and Sir Joshua Reynolds too, began, so they thought, with the evidence, and reached upwards to find a presiding principle. In doing so they got themselves out where the ice is thinnest – where Burke, blasting the abstractions of revolutionary France, decried 'the metaphysics of an undergraduate'; or where Reynolds, perhaps mindful of

Newton and Locke, insisted on 'rational firmness in the place of vain presumption'.[44] The dividing line between their informal principles and the *a priori* postulates of obnoxious republicans was narrower than Burke and Reynolds imagined. Still, they were altogether English in their insistence upon rational firmness and exposition solidly grounded on experience. The French, from simple, rationalistic premises like natural rights, reached forth to realize Liberty, Equality, and Fraternity – abstractions at once so sublime and terrifying that the guillotine had to work overtime to bring them to life by killing all sorts of people. The English built up, or at least persuaded themselves that they built up, their generalizations from complex and historical particulars. Burke dwelt not on Liberty but on specific English liberties. Dreading the unchecked will and appetite of the masses, he insisted on the rule of English law.

In truth, the young English gentleman

learned to walk and live within a Rotunda of law. The young gentleman was confronted with more laws than obtain even on a modern warship – laws of conduct, laws of strategy, and laws of tactics. For him as he grew up there were laws of etiquette and laws of taste in literature and the arts; there were also physical laws, statutory and common law, canon law, international law, the law of Scripture, and finally and above all, God's moral law for man, the Law of Nature itself. To this law, purely conceptual and broadly secular, no less than to physical law, the eighteenth century referred when it used that most popular phrase, 'the nature of things'. The nature of things, exalted above the merely accidental, was the necessary order of things.[45] No wonder man was the proper study – man in his relations with other men in society, in his relations with varying environments the world over, man in his relation to the Author of Nature. There was dignity in this search to understand law – the dignity of learning. It showed in precise statement, in that seriousness which blended so happily with wit and laughter, and in finish of expression. We think of Gibbon's luminous page, luminous from polish and because its reflections upon human conduct across the interminable ages instructed and therefore enlightened men. We think, too, of Johnson's Shakespeare who spoke the language not of poets but of men, as in *Othello*, 'the vigorous and vivacious offspring of observation impregnated by genius'. From Shakespeare's writings, Johnson concluded, 'a system of social duties may be selected, for he that thinks reasonably must think morally'.[46]

For what purpose, this dignity of learning and this attendance upon observation and experience? For one's enjoyment? To discover the truth of Aristotle's saying (which Johnson used to quote 'with great warmth') 'that there was the same difference between one learned and unlearned, as between the living and the dead'?[47] To do good, even as Latitudinarian preachers had always counselled? Or to promote the fitness of what we now term an élite both to govern and to influence the minds of men? If people still read Locke, as indeed they did, the stress on the aristocratic purpose of a gentleman's education was ready to hand; Locke's ends of a gentleman's education were four – virtue, wisdom, breeding, and learning. The four ends constituted a gentleman's character, and of them learning was the least part of education. 'The great business of all,' Locke said, 'is virtue and wisdom.' Virtue, to Locke, meant truthfulness, the love of God, and good nature towards others. Wisdom, why, wisdom was nothing more than Aristotle's 'practical' as opposed to his 'philosophic' wisdom: wisdom was 'for a man's managing his business ablely, and with fore-sight, in this world'. Integrity constituted the beginning of wisdom, and its later aspects were to be learned 'from time, experience and observation, and an acquaintance with men, their tempers, and designs'.[48] The ends of education were practical because they were profoundly humanistic.

Humanism in eighteenth-century England was a philosophy concerned with the fitness of the governing class. Humanism was the education of philosopher-kings (and queens) in an open aristocracy, that is to say, the education of men and women whose power was always to be checked and guided by their virtue and wisdom. English humanism had two purposes: service to society, including service to Church and State; and the cultivation of both mind and body to their full capacity in order to make a harmonious and active whole.

Englishmen of the eighteenth century never put their concept of humanism in these words. They took the definition but not the ideal for granted. To find the same meaning in the words of a contemporary we have only to turn to Burke. He wrote in 1791:

A true natural aristocracy is not a separate interest in the state, or separable from it. It is an essential integrant part of any large body rightly constituted . . . To be bred in a place of estimation . . . to be taught to respect one's self; to be habituated to the censorial inspection of the public eye; to look early to public opinion; to stand upon such elevated ground as to be enabled to take a large view of the widespread and infinitely diversified combinations of men and affairs in a large society; to have leisure to read, to reflect, to converse; to be enabled to draw the court and attention of the wise and learned, wherever they are to be found . . . to be taught to despise danger in pursuit of honor and duty . . . to be led to a guarded and regulated conduct, from a sense that you are considered as an instructor of your fellow-citizens in their highest concerns . . . to be employed as an administrator of law and justice, and to be thereby amongst the first benefactors to mankind. To be a professor of high science, or of liberal and ingenuous art; to be amongst rich traders, who from their success are presumed to have sharp and vigorous understandings . . . : These are the circumstances of men that form what I should call a *natural* aristocracy, without which there is no nation.[49]

How well the magic rhetoric conjures up the ideal world of Whigs and intellectuals whom poor, passionate Burke so much admired! How vain his sentiments appear in our world of mobs, of xenophobic national feeling, and of the people's democracies! Is the whole set-piece now obsolete because 'aristocratic'? Let us pause before delivering that conclusion. Despite reference to standing upon 'elevated ground' and to being 'amongst rich traders' the passage contains no tittle to suggest either a class shutting merit out or political, intellectual, and moral values that are not indispensable to the security and development of Western civilization today.

Burke exalted the idea of nation. He exalted it in terms of the humanists' tradition of contemplation and action. He would have agreed with John Mill when he argued that truth, to be kept bright, must be debated and be debated by people fit through education to debate. I need scarcely point out the urgency of our necessity to lead the West in its vast struggle for the survival and extension of our Greek, Roman, and Biblical values against the 'terrible simplifiers', whether children of Rousseau or of Marx and Lenin. Nor need I stress the on-coming tidal wave of population that threatens to overwhelm not only the means of subsistence but also the means of education and therefore of civilization. Do the Dark Ages, as has been asked, approach once more – this time with noise of radios, commercials, bulldozers, and more and more confused, unbridled children? And we, meanwhile, the troubled, over-specialized intellectuals, like hungry sheep we look up to political shepherds, so few of whom seem to have fed on the best that has been thought and lived. Unlike Victorian voters, we no longer have an open, political class of educated men and women trained to do the governing when we wish to call upon them for government. In the front line of politics we need many more men like Peel and Gladstone (both of them double-firsts at Oxford) and among the quicksands of diplomacy people trained as Canning and Palmerston trained themselves.

We go in fear, it seems, of a political élite lest such be undemocratic. Currently the word 'aristocracy' is taboo, and the word 'mediocrity' appears sometimes to be confused with the Word of God. There is little moral and intellectual health in us. Our education has too often been what is called progressive: it is soft. Latin and Greek, which used to toughen and also civilize a man's mind, are now almost discarded; history, again too often, has become a train-load of established 'facts' rattling down the rails to no place in particular. Most history text-books have nothing much to teach – certainly not the dignity of learning. Was not Whitehead expressing a humanist's truism when he said that 'Moral education is impossible apart from the habitual vision of greatness'?[50] So often we study 'facts' and 'movements'; so rarely we study men and women and how and why they chose to do one thing rather than another. Worst of all, we have set aside the education of a sense of responsibility and blunt duty in our quest for adjustment and private satisfaction.

We are passing from the many-sidedness of the great amateurs, the self-taught intellectuals. Why? Because, I suggest, the philosophy of individualism, the rise of the professions, the devastating questions asked of the past in the later nineteenth century, the prestige of pure and applied science have all led to specialization. 'And where,' Mr. G. M. Young asked in a famous passage,

> shall we look for the successors of the Mills and Ruskins and Tennysons? Or of the public for which they wrote? The common residual intelligence is becoming impoverished for the benefit of the specialist, the technician, and the aesthete: we leave behind us the world of historical ironmasters and banker historians, geological divines and scholar tobacconists, with its genial watchword: to know something of everything and everything of something . . . we go out into the Waste Land of Ex-

> perts, each knowing so much about so little that he can neither be contradicted nor is worth contradicting.[51]

We have reached a new Tower of Babel. We have lost the eighteenth-century sense of the order of things. Communists have their order of things. Our traditions, our appreciation of the complexities underlying truth, oblige us to reject the Communists' order of things. We decline to lie in the bed of Procrustes. Yet if we will only look, we shall see that we do have our order of things, an order clear and complete enough — despite the demolition squads of the last hundred years — to live by. Our order still consists of the inexorable laws of strategy, in government of the rule of law, and in society what ought to be the equally inexorable laws of conduct, in short, the austere cardinal virtues made lovely by our charity. And surely we need not believe political realists when they tell us that the historical process consists of unique and non-recurrent events. They were crying 'the past is the past' when Austria fell to the Nazis. 'We cannot say,' Churchill reminded them in that grave hour,' "The past is the past," without surrendering the future.'[52] The future was not surrendered because the future rested on 'brains', above all, on the moral will of the Allies. We, democrats that we are, have only to resolve that the future shall not be surrendered to the experts and the under-educated, but that the past shall live again when we educate a political and intellectual class to the idea of duty, and the thing, not without great difficulty, can be again.

The issue comes down to our schools, our colleges and universities, above all to our homes and families. The colleges and universities can do only so much. Splendid the ideal may be, but it does remain an open question whether most people can be educated in the course of one generation. For in education, like society itself, mind must conspire with mind. Time is required to produce, and so on. The job ultimately rests with families. But the families of wealth are not, it appears, producing in needed quantity the qualities of intellectual aristocracy. Indeed the most disturbing thing about too many of us in these trying times is the disparity between our wealth and our education. 'You cannot,' G. M. Young once remarked, 'educate people very much faster than you civilize their families.'[53]

NOTES

1. *Nicomachean Ethics,* I. 2. 1094[b].
2. Jacques Barzun, *The House of Intellect* (New York, 1959), p. 26.
3. Cf. N. McKendrick, 'Josiah Wedgwood: an Eighteenth-Century Entrepreneur in Salesmanship and Marketing Techniques', *Economic History Review,* Second Series, XII (1960), pp. 408-33.
4. *Politics,* IV. 8. 1294[a]; *Nicomachean Ethics,* II. 6. 1107[a].
5. Chesterfield to his Son, London, 10 Jan. O.S. 1749.
6. Alexis de Tocqueville, *Journeys to England and Ireland,* ed. J. P. Mayer (New Haven, 1958), p. 75.
7. Chesterfield to his Son, London, 9 Oct. O.S. 1747.
8. Sir Nathaniel Wraxall, *Historical Memoirs of My Own Times* (London, 1815), I, p. 155.
9. Cf. Mark H. Curtis, *Oxford and Cambridge in Transition, 1558-1642* (Oxford, 1959).
10. F. E. Brightman, *The English Rite* (London, 1915), II, 1053, 1028.
11. Sir Ernest Barker, 'The Education of the English Gentleman in the Sixteenth Century', *Traditions of Civility* (Cambridge, 1948), p. 145.
12. Lord Bristol to Carr Hervey, London, 27 June 1704. *Letter Books of John Hervey, First Earl of Bristol* (Wells, 1894), I, p. 203.
13. Bolingbroke to Lord Huntingdon, Battersea, 24 Oct. 1748. Historical Manuscripts Commission, *Hastings MSS.* (London, 1934), III, p. 65.
14. London, 2 June 1790. *The Correspondence of James Boswell and his Sons,* ed. Arthur W. Dixon (unpublished Yale dissertation, 1953).
15. *Transactions of the Society of Arts,* XVII (1799), pp. 119-39.

16. *Some Thoughts concerning Education,* § 1 and 'Epistle Dedicatory to Edward Clarke'.
17. *The Rambler,* no. 25, 12 June 1750.
18. Cleanth Brooks, 'The Country Parson as Research Scholar: Thomas Percy, 1760-1770', *Papers of the Bibliographical Society of America,* LIII (1959), pp. 222, 236.
19. Sir Lewis Namier, *The Structure of Politics at the Accession of George III,* 2nd. ed. (London, 1957), p. 39; cf. James M. Osborn, 'Travel Literature and the Rise of Neo-Hellenism in England', *Bulletin of the New York Public Library,* LXVII (1963), p. 288.
20. 'The Intellectual Aristocracy', *Studies in Social History. A Tribute to G. M. Trevelyan,* ed. J. H. Plumb (London, 1955), pp. 243-87. For criticisms of Annan's 'valuable' study see A. R. Wagner, *English Genealogy* (Clarendon Press, 1960), pp. 168, 173; and W. H. Dunham's review of Wagner in *Speculum,* Jan. 1961.
21. Paul Bloomfield, *Uncommon People. A Study of England's Elite* (London, 1955); W. T. J. Gun, *Studies in Hereditary Ability* (London, 1928). Among certain historians hereditary ability is currently *une vue de l'esprit.*
22. 'The Great Villiers Connection', *Essays and Sketches in Biography* (Meridian Books, 1956), pp. 291-3.
23. George Hay Drummond, *Sermons on Public Occasions . . . by Robert Late Archbishop of York* (Edinburgh, 1803), pp. xxvi-xxvii.
24. David Fordyce, *Dialogues Concerning Education* (London, 1745), pp. 61-2.
25. *Boswell's Life of Johnson,* ed. G. B. Hill and L. F. Powell (Oxford, 1934-50), V, pp. 108-9. Hereafter cited as *Life.*
26. *Annals of The Club* (London, 1914), pp. 134-53.
27. *ibid.,* pp. 39-40.
28. Samuel Johnson, *A Dictionary of the English Language, s. v.* club.

29. *Life,* IV, p. 179.
30. *ibid.,* p. 20.
31. *ibid.,* III, pp. 230-8.
32. Warren R. Dawson, ed., *The Banks Letters* (London, 1958), pp. vii-viii.
33. George Macaulay Trevelyan, *English Social History* (London, 1942), pp. 404-5.
34. John Locke, *An Essay Concerning Human Understanding,* ed. A. C. Fraser (Oxford, 1894), I, p. 14. Hereafter cited as *Essay.*
35. *Essay,* I, pp. 121-2.
36. Edwin Arthur Burtt, *The Metaphysical Foundations of Modern Physical Science* (London, 1949), p. 214.
37. *Essay,* I, pp. 30-1.
38. 'A Letter to a Noble Lord', *Works* (Boston, 1884), V, p. 189.
39. 'Personification Reconsidered', *New Light on Dr. Johnson,* ed. F. W. Hilles (New Haven, 1959), p. 224.
40. David C. Douglas, *English Scholars, 1660-1730* (London, 1951), chap. xiii.
41. *ibid.,* p. 283.
42. *Life,* I, p. 454.
43. 'Reflections on the Revolution in France', *Works* (Boston, 1884), III, pp. 457, 456.
44. *The Discourses of Sir Joshua Reynolds* (The World's Classics), p. 118.
45. Ernst Cassirer, *The Philosophy of the Enlightenment* (Princeton, 1951), p. 243; L. P. Curtis, 'Gibbon's Paradise Lost', in *The Age of Johnson. Essays Presented to Chauncey Brewster Tinker* (New Haven, 1949), p. 76.
46. 'Preface to Shakespeare', *Works* (Oxford, 1825), V, pp. 126-7, 115.
47. *Life,* IV, p. 13.

48. *Some Thoughts Concerning Education,* § § 200, 134-40.
49. 'An Appeal from the New to the Old Whigs', *Works* (Boston, 1884), IV, pp. 174-5.
50. A. N. Whitehead, 'The Place of Classics in Education', *The Aims of Education and Other Essays* (London, 1929), p. 106.
51. G. M. Young, *Victorian England. Portrait of an Age* (London, 1944), p. 160.
52. Winston S. Churchill, 'The Annexation of Austria, March 14, 1938', *While England Slept* (New York, 1938), p. 390.
53. G. M. Young, *Today and Yesterday* (London, 1948), p. 77.

JOHNSON'S CLUB

BY HERMAN W. LIEBERT

The whole concept of a club is one of the most English things in the world. The very word itself is English in origin, probably derived from the Anglo-Saxon *clifian,* to cleave, reflecting the essential fact about a club, that its expenses should be divided up among its members. Continental countries recognize the English origin of "club": French, German, Spanish, and Italian all use the English word, each perverting the word in its own outlandish, unEnglish fashion.

Argentina has roast beef; Nova Scotia has fog; the Pacific Northwest has salmon; Boston has the broad A – but, although there are clubs elsewhere to be sure, England is *par excellence* the land of clubs. It has been said that if three Englishmen were cast away on a desert isle, two of them would form a club to keep the third out. Not long after *The* Club was founded, some men who didn't belong to it established, magnificently oblivious of the rest of mankind, a second group; it was called, in perfect English simplicity, The Other Club.

The Englishness of club life has persisted into our own day. It was not long ago that *Punch* printed the announcement: "The Athenaeum has been closed for repainting and repairs; but before the re-opening all members will be replaced in their original positions." And George Moore wisely observed, "No place in England where *everyone* can go is considered respectable."

The Club, is, I think, the most extraordinary phenomenon among all the clubs that have ever been. It began with eight members, and these eight included the best painter of the age, Reynolds; the best prose writer, Johnson; the pre-eminent political philosopher, Burke; the greatest poet and dramatist, Goldsmith; one of the best classical scholars, Langton; and one of the best book-collectors, Beauclerk. That's a pretty high average for a total of only eight.

Ten years later, the membership had been increased to sixteen, and there had been added to those already mentioned the chief antiquarian of the day, Percy; Blackstone's successor as professor of law, Robert Chambers; England's greatest actor, Garrick; the greatest linguist of the age, William Jones; and the man destined to be the world's greatest biographer, Boswell.

Ten years later still, by the year of Johnson's death, the membership had been increased to thirty-five. And there had been elected the other great statesman, Fox; the unrivalled historian, Gibbon; the political economist, Adam Smith; the greatest living dramatist, Sheridan (poor Goldsmith being dead); the president of the Royal Society, Banks;

the great maritime and international lawyer, William Scott, later Lord Stowell; the first president of the Roxborough Club and owner of the fabulous Althorp library, the 2nd Earl Spencer; the greatest Shakespearean editor, Edmond Malone; the poet laureate, Thomas Warton; the chief historian of music, Burney; and the most successful physician, Richard Warren.

Forty-four men were members of The Club between its founding and Johnson's death twenty years later; twenty-one of them were the first men of their day in their respective fields. I think that is an extraordinary record.

If the head of the membership touched the clouds, it must be admitted that at the other end there were some pedal extremities suspiciously like clay.

Samuel Dyer, for example, was very highly regarded by his fellow members, but his excellencies have not endured. Percy told Malone that everyone at The Club had such a high opinion of Dyer's knowledge and respect for his judgment as to appeal to him constantly, and that his verdict was final. When Johnson read to The Club a Latin epitaph he had written, Dyer asked him to read it over again, and then pointed out a mistake, which Johnson at once accepted. That is not one's usual view of Dr. Johnson. At The Club, when Goldsmith was rattling away about music, another member asked Dyer's opinion, which he gave with great precision. "Why," said Goldsmith, "you seem to know a good deal of this matter!" "If I had not," Dyer replied, "I should not in this company have said a word upon the subject,"—a lesson poor Goldsmith never managed to learn.

Yet Dyer was so lazy that he never finished any of the two or three small literary projects he undertook, and lived close to starvation rather than exert himself. He finally did finish the revision of an earlier edition of Plutarch, but then he inherited £8,000, invested it very unwisely at Dr. Johnson's advice, and lost every penny. He died soon afterward, leaving too little to pay for his funeral.

Agmondesham Vesey, M.P., is another of less than immortal fame. He was accountant-general for Ireland, and later an Irish privy councillor, but he creeps into the DNB only as the second husband of Mrs. Vesey, the notable bluestocking, who held salons for the ladies the same night that The Club met, to which the gentlemen would later repair. Mr. Vesey seems to have been so bland that even his own wife failed to remember him. Though he *was* her second husband, Mrs. Vesey spoke very harshly one night of a lady who had re-married. A friend quietly reminded her of her own status. "Bless me, my dear," Mrs. Vesey exclaimed, "I had quite forgotten it."

And then there is Dr. George Fordyce, not one of the most celebrated but certainly one of the most human members of The Club. A physician of some success, he seldom went to bed, was accustomed to deliver his medical lectures in yesterday's clothes, having stayed up all night; drank oceans; and ate but once a day on the theory that a single meal was healthy. The scene of that single meal is a memorable one. For twenty years Fordyce ate at Dolly's Chophouse in Paternoster Row, at 4 o'clock precisely. The waiter would signal his arrival to the chef, who put a pound and a half of rump steak on the gridiron; the waiter meanwhile brought a tankard of strong ale, a bottle of port, and a quarter-pint of brandy. While the steak was cooking, Fordyce would have an appetizer – half a chicken, or a whole fish, washed down with half of his brandy. Then, with the steak, the ale, then the whole bottle of port, and then the rest of the brandy. It is not surprising that, when he was called to a fashionable lady patient one evening, he was too tipsy to count her pulsebeats. "Drunk, by God," he muttered, and left the house. While he was wondering next morning how to explain his behavior, her footman arrived with a message. "I know from what you said last night," she wrote, "that you discovered my unfortunate condition. I entreat you to keep the matter a secret between us in consideration of the enclosed" – which was a banknote of one hundred pounds.

Charles James Fox was another high liver. He was a notable liberal, who fought, when it was dangerous to fight, against the taxes that led to the American Revolution, against slavery, and against persecution of Dissenters and Roman Catholics, and he was by intellect worthy of membership in The Club. His political aplomb is well illustrated by his description of Napoleon after several interviews: "a young man considerably intoxicated with success." But when Fox relaxed, he did so with unJohnsonian license. When he was one of the Lords of the Treasury (and not yet twenty-five years old) he began a gambling session at Almack's club, where the smallest chips were £50. He played for nearly 24 hours without stopping; in a single hour before he quit, he won back £12,000 he had previously lost, but still owed £10,000 when he finished. Next day he spoke in Parliament, went to dinner at half past eleven at night, drank at White's club until seven in the morning, returned to Almack's and won £6,000 at the tables, and then went off to the races at Newmarket, where he lost another £10,000. One of his gambling sessions at Brookes's lasted from ten one night until six the next afternoon, and a club waiter stood by the table to tell the players whose deal it was, they being too sleepy to know for themselves.

Sir Thomas Charles Bunbury was one of the handsomest young men of his day, who kept a seat in Parliament warm for forty-three years. His real love was racing, and he was the winner of the very first Derby. He was less successful with that high-spirited filly, his wife, Lady Sarah Lennox, who left him two months after bearing under his roof the child of her cousin, Sir William Gordon.

But even these men, some of them obscure, some far from other members of The Club in intellectual stature, still had one common characteristic: they were agreeable, social beings, fit to be described by the word Johnson introduced into the language: they were eminently clubable.

What were the meetings of this Club like? Well, for the first few years the members met every Monday night at about seven or eight, and had supper together. This meal was only a light collation — usually cold meat and cheese, washed down with wine and punch. Dinner, the main meal of the day, was at this time usually taken at three or four in the afternoon. In 1772, the day was changed to Friday, and the members dined together every other week during the sitting of Parliament. The meal was now a real 18th-century repast: a soup, perhaps of green peas; then a stewed fish, accompanied by beans, bacon, salad, and a light meat course, such as veal or tripe; then roasted capons, with or without a beef dish as well, a veal dish, a venison pie, and sometimes stewed rabbits; and an ice or fruit for dessert. Dr. Nugent, Burke's father-in-law, had to content himself with a mere omelet, being a Roman Catholic, and Johnson sometimes fasted similarly: when he saw an omelet soon after Nugent died, he exclaimed, with tears in his eyes, "Ah, dear friend, I shall never eat an omelet with thee again."

Besides claret and port, which were to be had in profusion, there was punch, which was a favorite of Johnson's, made of wine or brandy, lemons or oranges, sugar, and water. For some years Johnson did not take spirits, and made his own non-alcoholic punch. But he was always aware of the social usefulness of drink, and in one of his essays compares the ingredients of punch to those of good conversation. "The spirit," he wrote, "volatile and fiery, is the proper emblem of vivacity and wit; the acidity of the lemon will very aptly figure pungency of raillery, and acrimony of censure; sugar is the natural representative of luscious adulation and gentle complaisance; and water is the proper hierogliphick of easy prattle, innocent and tasteless."

One of the most agreeable habits of The Club was that of keeping track, not of how much liquor was consumed, but of how much was left at the end of each meeting. Though The Club met at a tavern, first the Turk's Head, then at Prince's, and later at Baxter's, it maintained its own supply of potables.

The conversation ranged over every conceivable topic, and with talkers like Johnson, to say nothing of other members of The Club, it was often a headlong steeplechase, with every man for himself and the devil take the hindmost. In this free and equal society, where intellect rather than rank was the standard, no holds were barred; you will remember Boswell's remark when Johnson said they had had good talk the night before: "Yes, Sir, you tossed and gored several persons."

Such was the intellectual calibre of The Club that any topic could be expertly discussed. When it was proposed that the number of members should be increased, Goldsmith favored the step: "It would give agreeable variety to our meetings," he said unwarily, "for there can be nothing new among us; we have travelled over each other's minds." That was too much for Johnson. "Sir," he growled, "you have not travelled over *my* mind, I promise you."

Goldsmith could not keep up with this or other conversational crises, but when he had his pen in his hand, he made up for it. His poem *Retaliation* contains epitaphs on a number of members of The Club, written as if they were already dead, though he himself was the first member to die after it was composed.

Here is part of the pretended epitaph on Garrick, and it is hard to deny that Goldsmith had the last word:

> Here lies David Garrick, describe me who can,
> An abridgement of all that was pleasant in man . . .
> On the stage he was natural, simple, affecting,
> 'Twas only that when he was off he was acting . . .
> Though secure of our hearts, yet confoundedly sick
> If they were not his own by finessing and trick,
> He cast off his friends, as a huntsman his pack,
> For he knew when he pleas'd he could whistle them back.
> Of praise a mere glutton, he swallow'd what came,
> And the puff of a dunce he mistook it for fame;
> Till his relish grown callous, almost to disease,
> Who pepper'd the highest was surest to please.

But even Goldsmith could not manage

anything harsh about Reynolds, who seems by general agreement to have been the kindest and sweetest character of the whole group. His epitaph is:

> Here Reynolds is laid, and to tell you my
>   mind,
> He has not left a better or wiser behind:
> His pencil was striking, resistless and grand;
> His manners were gentle, complying, and
>   bland;
> Still born to improve us in every part,
> His pencil our faces, his manners our heart:
> To coxcombs averse, yet most civilly
>   steering,
> When they judg'd without skill he was still
>   hard of hearing:
> When they talk'd of their Raphaels,
>   Correggios, and stuff,
> He shifted his trumpet, and only took snuff.

Sometimes the conversational going got really rocky. Dr. Barnard, later Bishop of Killaloe, one evening asserted that men seldom improved after the age of forty-five. Johnson, who was in his sixties, and still desperately hoped for improvement, differed. Barnard persisted, at which Johnson observed, "I do not say that there are not some exceptions; pray, Sir, how old are you?" But Barnard won the exchange after all, for he wrote some verses on the subject, including these lines:

I lately thought no man alive
Could e'er improve past forty-five,
  And ventured to assert it;
The observation was not new,
But seemed to me so just and true
  That none could controvert it.

"No, Sir," says Johnson, " 'tis not so;
That's your mistake and I can show
  An instance, if you doubt it.
You, Sir, who are near forty-eight
May *much* improve, 'tis not too late;
  I wish you'd set about it"...

Let Johnson teach me how to place
In fairest light each borrow'd grace,
  From him I'll learn to write;
Copy his clear, familiar style,
And from the roughness of his file,
  Grow, like himself, polite.

When one starts to talk about The

Club, or indeed about almost anything else in the second half of the 18th century, he soon finds that he has been slowly and imperceptibly led to talk about Johnson. I do not think this is merely my own preoccupation with the man; I think it is both indicative and inevitable. The fact is that because he is by so much the most forcible personality, the most commanding presence, the most stimulating mind, even among this constellation of giants, it is impossible not to be drawn to him as the center of the circle. The members of The Club felt this themselves. Burke and Langton were walking home one night from The Club, when Burke observed that Johnson's talk had been very great; Langton agreed, but indicated he would have liked to hear more of Burke's conversation. "Oh, no," said Burke, "it is enough for me to have rung the bell to him." This was not false modesty: nor is Burke himself so little a figure as to be suited only for sitting at Johnson's feet. It is Burke of whom one contemporary said that Gibbon might have been cut out of a corner of Burke's mind without his missing it. These men, for all their own brilliance, felt the irresistible pull of Johnson's intellect, and we today respond to the same influence that draws us to him as the central figure.

I do not mean to imply that all was love and kisses in The Club, even toward Johnson himself. When Lord Charlemont retired to Ireland, and no longer attended meetings of The Club, Beauclerk wrote to him, "If you do not come here, I will bring all the Club over to Ireland, to live with you and *that* will drive you here in your own defense. Johnson shall spoil all your books; Goldsmith pull up all your flowers, and Boswell talk to you; stay there if you can." When Adam Smith was elected, Boswell wrote to a friend, "Smith is now of our Club. It has lost its select merit." And Johnson himself was sometimes acid about his fellow-members. Of Bishop Shipley's attendance at The Club, he said, "A Bishop has nothing to do at a tippling house. There is nothing immoral in it. But a Bishop should not go to a house where he may meet a man leading out a whore."

These men, almost all of them, were of such power and character and originality of mind that there were bound to be clashes of personality; indeed, it is just those fireworks that make the accounts of The Club's meetings such good reading. Here is Boswell's report of one meeting of The Club, from his original manuscript since it contains a few details that were not printed in the published *Life:*[1]

Friday April 7 I dined with [Johnson] at the Literary Club which had now undergone a change to the better that on the first friday of every month we should dine together instead of meeting in the evening. Johnson: I have been reading Twiss's Travels in Spain, which are just

[1]This and the passage below are printed by permission of Yale University and the McGraw-Hill Book Co. The transcriptions are *verbatim*.

come out. They are as good as the first book of travels that you will take up. They are as good as those of Keysler or Blainville, nay, as Addison's, if you take out the learning. Beauclerk said, they are nothing without the learning . . . [Johnson] I have not indeed cut the leaves yet, but I have read in them where the pages are open, and I do not suppose that what is on the pages which are closed is worse than what is on the open pages. It would seem that Addison had not acquired much Italian learning . . . I mentioned Addison's having borrowed many of his learned remarks from Leandro Alberti. Mr. Beauclerk said it was alleged that he had borrowed also from another Italian author. Johnson: Why, sir, all who go to look for what the classicks have said of Italy must find the same passages; and I should think it was one of the first things the Italians would do on the revival of learning to collect all that the Roman authors had said of their country. Ossian being mentioned, Johnson: Supposing the Irish and Erse languages to be the same, which I do not believe, yet as there is no reason to suppose that the inhabitants of the highlands and hebrides ever wrote their native language, it is not to be credited that a long poem was preserved among them. If we had no evidence of the art of writing being practiced in one of the counties of England we should not believe that long poem was preserved there, though in the neighboring counties where the same language was spoken the inhabitants could write. Beauclerk: The ballad of Lillabullero was once in the mouths of all the people of this country and is said to have had a great effect in bringing about the Revolution, yet I question whether any body can repeat it now, which shews how improbable it is that much poetry should be preserved by tradition. Dr. Percy mentioned an internal objection to the antiquity of the poetry said to be Ossian's that we do not find the wolf in it, which must have been the case had it been of that age. The mention of the wolf had led Johnson to think of other wild beasts; and while Sir Joshua Reynolds and Mr. Langton were carrying on a dialogue about something which engaged them earnestly, he in the midst of it broke out "Pennant tells of bears" (I forget what) They went on; while he being dull of hearing did not perceive it, or if he did was not willing to mind them. So he continued to roar out his remarks, and Bear (like a word in a catch, as Beauclerk said) was repeatedly heard at intervals, which coming from him who by those who did not know him had been so often assimilated to that ferocious animal while we who were sitting around could hardly stifle laughter, produced a very ludicrous effect. Silence having ensued, he proceeded, "We are told that the black bear is innocent, but I should not like to engage with him." Mr. Gibbon muttered in a low voice "I should not like to engage with *you*." This though ironically meant, was a judicious truth if applied to a competition of abilities. Patriotism having become one of our topicks, Johnson suddenly uttered in a strong determined tone an apophthegm at which many will start. Patriotism is the last refuge of a scoundrel. But let it be considered that he did not mean a real and generous love for our country, but that pretended patriotism of which Great Britain has seen too much. Some of us maintained that all patriots were not scoundrels, and a gentleman urged (not by Johnson) to name one, an eminent person whom we all greatly admired [Burke] was mentioned. Johnson: Sir, I do not say that he is not honest. But we have no reason to conclude from his political conduct that he *is* honest. Were he to accept of a place in this ministry, he would lose that character for firmness which he has, and might be turned out of his place in a year . . . Mrs. Pritchard being mentioned, he said, Her playing was quite mechanical. It is wonderful how little mind she had. Sir, she had never read the tragedy of Macbeth all through. She no more thought of the play out of which her part was taken than a shoemaker thinks of the skin out of which the piece of leather of which he is making a pair of shoes is cut . . . [And so on.]

Here, in one short part of an evening, we have had talk of travel books, ancient poetry, politics, and the stage, to say nothing of the comic scene of the bear. It is no wonder that men of eminence were glad to be proposed for membership and that they were even more happy when they received the news that they had been elected. One blackball was sufficient to exclude, and the list of those rejected is almost as notable as those who were taken in, for it includes the first Earl Camden, who was Lord Chancellor at the time; Gibbon, who was blackballed early in 1774, when proposed by Goldsmith, but accepted on a second try; Lord Palmerston, also successful on a second try; and Dr. Porteus, the Bishop of London.

Boswell himself was anxious about his election, and has left us a vivid account of the evening when his name came up. It is clear that Johnson forced the issue, for he told Boswell later that several members were against him, but, added Johnson, "they knew that if they refused you, they'd probably never have got in another. I'd have kept them all out." The night his name was to be voted on, Boswell stayed behind at Beauclerk's house while Johnson, Reynolds, and other members went off to the meeting. This is again from the original manuscript of the *Life of Johnson:*

The gentlemen went away to the Club, and I was left at Beauclerk's till the fate of my election should be announced to me, and as one blackball excluded, I sat in anxious suspense and even the charms of Lady Diana Beauclerk's conversation could hardly relieve me. Mr. Beauclerk's coach returned for me in less than an hour with a note from him that I was chosen. I question if any election could give me a higher sensation. I hastened to the Turk's Head in Gerard Street, and was introduced to such a society as can seldom be found. Mr. Edmund Burke whom I then saw for the first time, and whose splendid talents had long made me ardently wish for his acquaintance; Dr. Nugent, Mr. Garrick, Dr. Goldsmith, Mr., now Sir William Jones and the company with whom I had dined. Upon my entrance, Johnson who had proposed me as a member, placed himself behind a chair on which he leant as on a desk or pulpit, and with humorous formality gave me a charge, pointing out the duties incumbent upon me as a good member of this club.

An even older friend of Johnson's than Boswell came very close to trouble in his candidacy. Soon after The Club was formed, Reynolds mentioned it to Garrick, who remarked, "I like it much; I think I shall be of you." When Johnson heard of this, in spite of his long friendship with Garrick, he took fire. "He'll be of us," said Johnson, "How does he know we will permit him. The first duke in England has no right to hold such language." It was nearly ten years until Garrick was proposed, but when he was, Johnson supported him warmly, he was elected, and when Garrick died six years later, Johnson insisted that there should be a year's widowhood before a successor was chosen.

Sir William Jones, who knew twenty-eight languages, wrote of The Club in 1780 that there was no branch of human knowledge on which some of its members were not capable of giving information, and Boswell and Johnson amused themselves, on their tour of the Hebrides, by drawing up an imaginary college with a faculty made up wholly of Club members. Boswell was to teach civil and Scots law; Chambers, English law; Burke, politics and eloquence; Garrick, public speaking; Langton, Greek; Colman, Latin; Dr. Nugent, medicine; Lord Charlemont, modern history; Sir William Jones, Oriental languages; Goldsmith, poetry and ancient history; Reynolds, painting; Percy, practical divinity and antiquities; and Johnson himself logic, metaphysics, and scholastic divinity. Poor Mr. Vesey was put down to teach Celtic, a subject of which he was wholly innocent, though he could have taught architecture in a pinch. Johnson lamented that since the death of Dyer they did not have a good mathematician. Short of this, however, The Club could have put forward a college that would have been the envy of any age.

But even this remarkable reservoir of intellectuality, even the fact that in Boswell The Club had a good reporter, and even the enduring attraction of Johnson, do not seem enough among them to justify the kind of attention that has been paid to The Club almost since its beginning. Why, then, does The Club seem so important?

Some of the reasons Mr. Curtis has already presented. I would like to indicate some additional, or rather parallel reasons.

He emphasized the degree to which The Club was a society of innate merit. We have already heard Johnson say that the first duke in England could not presume to membership. This was a group of minds, on the whole, that would have commanded attention anywhere. Even judged by the way merit was rewarded in their own time, the members of The Club showed their quality. Of the forty-four members in Johnson's lifetime, nineteen, or a little less than half, bore titles by the end of their lives. Of these, seven were inherited. But twelve of the members were raised to rank on their own merits.

What must also be recognized is the kind of merit The Club itself counted as important. This was not what the King or the world chose to reward. Dyer made no public impression; he was indeed so little moved by ambition that his talents can truly be said to have been wasted.

But he exercised his intellect with his intellectual equals – at The Club. This is also true of Langton, of Beauclerk, of Nugent, of Vesey, and of Chamier. Everyone likes to think that he too could have held up his head in this circle.

The freedom that The Club afforded its members in its meetings must also be appreciated. Here, within a society that was still a hierarchy first of birth, and only beginning to be a culture of accomplishment rewarded, the members of The Club could meet without reserve. The Lord, the Bishop, the Privy Councillor, met on intellectually common terms with the sons of provincial booksellers and schoolmasters. And if he who had the bluest blood did not also have the most cogent arguments, he lost the exchange.

In other words, by its mixed social complexion, its own standards of merit, and the freedom its members felt toward each other, The Club was in fact a true democracy. This, I am sure, is one of the reasons it appeals to us today, for we feel that, after centuries in which power equated with birth, and creative ability existed by royal or noble patronage only, we come into the fresh air of the age of Johnson and feel that for the first time we are in an atmosphere familiar to us, in which a man can make his own way, and rise quite to the top if his powers of achievement are sufficient. This is true of Johnson's age in general, and it is in particular true of The Club as a vivid and palpable microcosm of its time.

We find The Club, then, attractive to us because it had a kind of freedom that we share. But even more, I think, do we find the second half of the 18th century, and The Club as a symbol of it, deeply satisfying to us because of something it possessed that we desperately lack, and reach toward nostalgically. Johnson's was the last age in which it was possible for a single man even to try to encompass a substantial part of human knowledge, to have in any sense a universal mind. When, in the next age, it became impossible, man rebelled against intellect as such, and passed into a romantic period in which feeling was all-important. And from that day to this, man has remained more concerned with himself, his feelings, the world of his own experience and its impact on his senses, than with the broader examination of man and his world and the synthesis of general principles and general conclusions.

The intellectuals of the age of Johnson, the members of The Club, believed that general principles and general conclusions were still within man's grasp. The Round Robin that the members of The Club sent to Johnson protested his use of Latin instead of English in his epitaph on Goldsmith. One recalls, to be sure, that no one dared to sign his name first, and the round-robin form was adopted so that Johnson could not know who had started the protest. And they were right to be afraid; when he received it, Johnson snorted, "I wonder that Joe Warton, a scholar by profession, should be such a fool." Langton, the classical scholar, refused to sign. The epitaph, *in Latin,* may still be seen in Westminster Abbey. But what it is important to note is that some men, Johnson among them, still believed in Latin as the universal language of cultivated men, and this was almost the last moment when that view could be held; today it persists only in scientific nomenclature, in diplomas, in liturgy, and in numerals on cornerstones, for we have given up the hope that man's mind can encompass much more than one corner of human knowledge.

What Johnson was always doing in his writing, Reynolds was doing in painting, Burke in political philosophy, Gibbon in history, Smith in economics, and Stowell in international law: to refine and distill out of the past the essence of the best for the benefit of the future. "It is always a writer's duty to make the world better," Johnson wrote, and added, "he that thinks reasonably must think morally."

How different is our world, and how solid and reassuring Johnson's world seems to us as we look back to it.

Our American society seems paradoxically to have made man more lonely by making him merely a member of a mass. In Johnson's time one could afford to be an individual, could feel, in the strength that comes from a consciousness of the great past, that as its present spear-point he had individual importance. To-day, without support from tradition, we have been fractionated into so many units, no one of any peculiar external importance, that we can measure our satisfaction, our achievement, our reason for being, only in terms of some sort of norm, where we find safety in likeness with others while desperately struggling to preserve our unlikeness, our own personalities. The survival of our own personalities requires in us a degree of self-absorption, of concern in our own experiences and our own destinies, that is the mortal enemy of broad observation, broad generalization, broad concern for the way the whole present, *our* present, can grow out of the past and into the future.

The members of The Club, in contrast to this inward-looking orientation, felt firm confidence in the powers of the intellect, and were thus able to accept the corollary responsibility that the reasonable man owed to his society his best efforts to make it better – not to lick his own wounds or to appeal to a higher power for compassion, but to fight and to feel sure that reasonable men would fight alongside him for the general principles in which he believed. I need only recall the central figures of a hundred novels of the last ten years, none of them decisive enough to serve as the hero of a narrative of action based on principles, all of them soft, wheedling, and importunate of "understanding" which is the only way they can find to feel like whole human beings.

An observer who stands roughly half

way between the time of Johnson and our own saw this with what seems to me a paralyzing clarity. This is from Tocqueville in 1840.

"As social equality spreads, there are more and more people who, though neither so rich nor so powerful as to dominate their fellow-citizens, have nevertheless enough education and wealth to be self-sufficient. They owe nothing to anyone, and expect nothing from anyone; they have become accustomed to thinking of themselves as standing entirely on their own feet, and wholly in control of their destinies.

"Thus does democracy make every man forget that in the great scheme of things he is derived from his ancestors, and can survive only in his descendants; it separates him even from the other members of his own generation; it throws him always back upon his own resources, and threatens finally to wall him up in the solitude of his own consciousness."

That seems to me to speak eloquently

and accurately of our present dilemma. It explains why the beatniks feel beat and the angry young men feel angry, and the alone generation feels alone, and why all of them feel sorry for themselves and want us to feel sorry for them too. It explains why all of us have moments when, in spite of relative happiness and relative security, we face, perhaps at night and alone, those frightening questions of whether we believe in what we are, and whether the ends to which we devote so much frantic energy have any objective value or are likely to have any enduring results.

I do not pretend to know the answers, even for myself. But I do know that in the second half of the 18th century there were men who had found answers to those questions in which they could believe.

Their answers lay in the confidence they had in the power of the human mind. It is fashionable today to emphasize the limitations of the human mind, the ways in which it can deceive itself and hide from itself unpalatable truths. I do not intend to espouse "the power of positive thinking." And yet I believe it is worth remembering that the human mind which can deceive itself is the same human mind which has the power to uncover its self-deception and to reconstruct a world in which self-respect is achievable and a trust in the objective worth of human effort can be confidently maintained.

This, I believe, was the strength of those at the end of the 18th century — the members of The Club and similarly the men who founded our republic — who lived just at the moment when the old shackles of autocratic state and church were being thrown off, and before the new shackles of mass rule and average standards and the great grey sickness of the soul descended.

The Club, it seems to me, is a brilliant manifestation of this triumph of the aristocracy of the mind, and that is why The

Club seems important and attractive to us today — as an association dedicated to the nobler things of the human spirit, a group in which the qualities of mind prevailed rather than those old ones of social and financial position on the one hand, or the debased new standards of the common man on the other. And it is just because these principles will always appeal to men in every generation wise enough to assign the proper, supreme value to the power of intellect that Johnson's club has achieved what it hoped for in its motto: *Esto Perpetua, May it last forever.*

APPENDIX

The members of The Club from its founding in 1764 until Johnson's death in 1784 were:

Samuel Johnson
Sir Joshua Reynolds
Edmund Burke
Christopher Nugent
Bennet Langton
Topham Beauclerk
Oliver Goldsmith
Anthony Chamier
Sir John Hawkins
Samuel Dyer
Thomas Percy, Bishop of Dromore
Sir Robert Chambers
George Colman
James Caulfield, Viscount Charlemont
David Garrick
Sir William Jones
Agmondesham Vesey
James Boswell
Charles James Fox

APPENDIX

Sir Charles Bunbury
George Fordyce
George Steevens
Edward Gibbon
Adam Smith
Thomas Barnard, Bishop of Limerick
Joseph Warton
Richard Brinsley Sheridan
John Fitzpatrick, Earl of Upper Ossory
Richard Marlay, Bishop of Waterford and Lismore
John Dunning, Baron Ashburton
Sir Joseph Banks
William Windham
William Scott, Lord Stowell
George John Spencer, Earl Spencer
Jonathan Shipley, Bishop of St. Asaph
Edward Eliot, Lord Eliot
Edmond Malone
Thomas Warton
Charles Bingham, Earl of Lucan
Richard Burke
Sir William Hamilton
Henry Temple, Viscount Palmerston
Charles Burney
Richard Warren